The Usborne
GIRLS'
Activity
Book

Written by

Lucy Bowman, Rebecca Gilpin,
James Maclaine and Louie Stowell

Designed and illustrated by

Erica Harrison, Katie Lovell, Caroline Day, Emily Beevers,
Lauren Ellis, Antonia Miller and Jan McCafferty

Edited by Fiona Watt

You'll find the answers and solutions
to the puzzles on pages 92-96.

In the park

It's a busy day at the park and there are lots of things to spot. Draw circles around everything you find.

There are seven people wearing sunglasses. Can you spot them?

Can you see six girls in red spotted dresses?

Look for two people taking photos.

There is one red balloon. Can you find it?

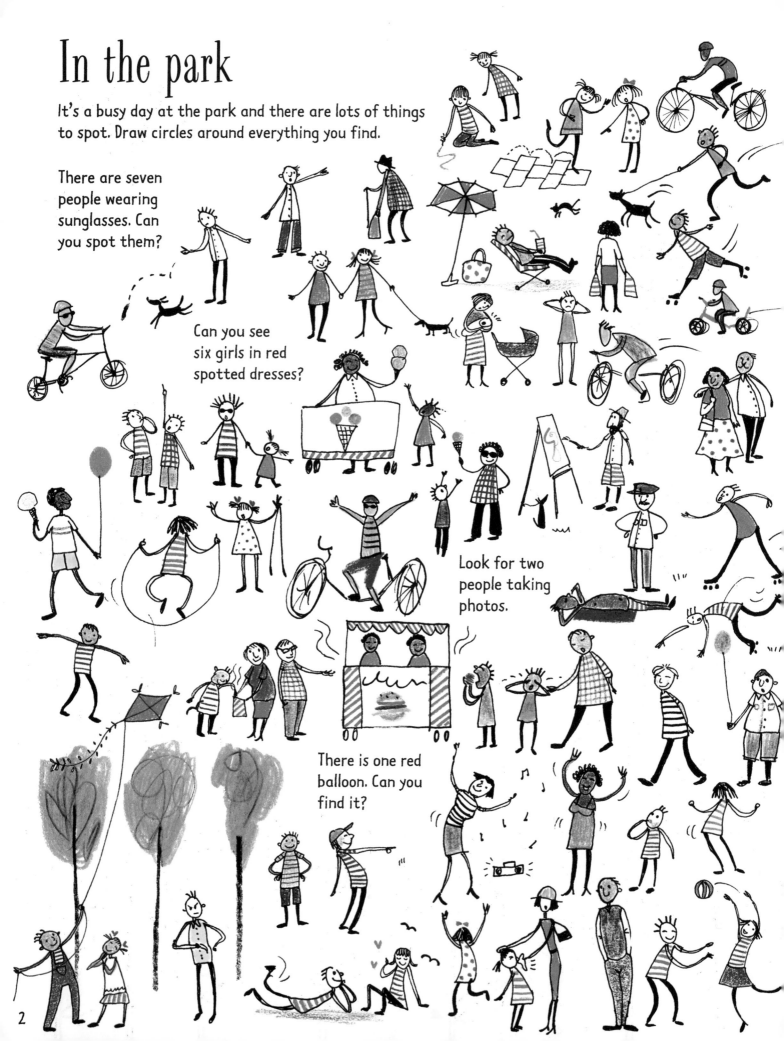

2

Can you find eight cyclists?

Look for two beach balls.

Can you spot five dogs?

What else can you find?

3

Doodle

more flowers and plants,
then fill them in...

'Patchwork' flowers

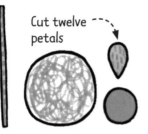
Cut twelve petals

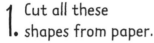

1. Cut all these shapes from paper.

2. Glue the stalk onto a piece of paper, then add the other shapes.

3. Glue on the leaves, then draw 'stitches' with a pencil or pen.

You could add more butterflies and bees to this picture...

DID YOU KNOW? Young sunflowers face the sun in the morning and turn around to follow it all day. Once the flowers are fully grown, they stop rotating, and most of them face in the direction of the morning sun.

Fun in the rain

Even though it's raining, lots of people have gone into town to do some shopping.
Help to brighten up their day by decorating their umbrellas...

Doodle
more clouds in the sky.

Add some raindrops, too.

THE RAIN CLOUD GAME

One person says a word...

RAIN

Someone else says a word that they associate with that word...

CLOUD

The next person says a word that links up with the second word...

SKY

...and so on. If anyone repeats a word or can't think of a new word, they're out of the game.

SHOPPING LIST PUZZLE

This list has been dropped in a puddle, and now it's all mixed-up. Can you work out what should be on it?

DREBA   ....

KILM   ....

ESHECE   ....

TELUCTE   ....

AANABN   ....

Count the raindrops

Fill them in as you go...

...and do any sums here:

TOTAL:.............

Puddle-jumping

Help this girl jump in as many puddles as possible on her way home. Without going over any paths twice, draw a line along the route with the most puddles:

7

Sparkling jewels

Stop, thief!

A thief has stolen a bag of loot from 'Dazzling Gems'. Draw a line to show his getaway route, avoiding dangers on the way.

Dazzling Gems

Grrr!

POLICE

Which of the crowns below is missing a jewel? Add the missing jewel, then fill in the crowns, if you like...

A.

B.

C.

D.

8

Princess puzzle

Can you help these three princesses to share their gems? Izzy is the youngest, Jess the oldest, and Bella the one in the middle. For each gem that Izzy gets, Bella gets two and Jess gets three. Draw the number of gems that each girl should get, crossing them off as you go...

Jess

Bella

Izzy

Missing beads

Each of these necklaces has lost a bead! Figure out which shape of bead is missing from each necklace, then draw it on:

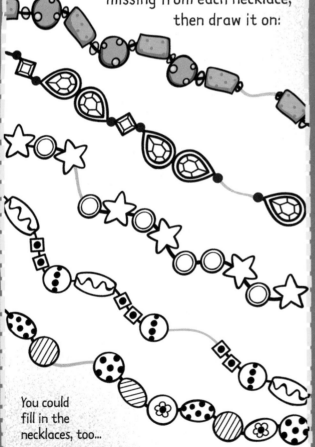

You could fill in the necklaces, too...

Can you find these gem-related words inside this ring? They go across, up and down, and some may even be backwards...

DIAMOND   GEMS   RUBY
EMERALD   JEWELS   SAPPHIRE

Cross off the words as you find them...

```
    G U E D O
  M T R H I E J
I S A P P H I R E
S A P G E N R K D M A
U G P D N O M A I D F
C E R L W H X C D V G
E M Z A F J E W E L S
K S J R C T R L U D P
O H E X D U S N S
  A M Q I B E A
    E J M Y R
```

Butterflies and flowers

Fill in the butterflies and flowers
below using warm shades, such as
reds, oranges and yellows...

Use cool shades for the butterflies and flowers on this page, such as blues, purples and greens....

Doodle more butterflies and add patterns on their wings.

11

Princess rescue maze

A princess has been imprisoned in her castle by a wicked witch, and a prince has come to save her. Help him find a safe path to the princess, avoiding all the perils in his way... including flapping bats and a sleeping dragon.

FOODY FUN

Draw faces on these fruits and vegetables...

DID YOU KNOW?

BANANAS grow with their pointed ends facing UP, so they look as if they're 'upside-down'.

POPCORN isn't a modern invention. Popped corn from around 5,600 years ago has been found in a cave in New Mexico.

EGGS float in water if they've gone bad, so if an egg floats, don't eat it!

We're fruit!

TOMATOES are used like vegetables in cooking, but they are actually the *fruit* of the tomato plant...

The letters on these cans, boxes and jars are mixed up – can you put them into the correct order?

 YEHON
....

 SMOTEOTA
....

 LUROF
....

 SKIEOCO
....

 ARCLEE
....

 TAPSA
....

Eat the alphabet game (play this with a friend or two)

Take turns thinking of foods that begin with A, then B, then C, then D...
Here's an example of how it works:

I'm so hungry, I could eat an apricot.

I'm so hungry, I could eat an apricot and some blueberries.

I'm so hungry, I could eat... an apricot, some blueberries and a cake!

Continue until someone forgets something on the list, or can't think of something that begins with the next letter. Some letters (Q, X, Z) are really hard, so agree which letters to leave out before you start.

QUICK AND EASY 'PIZZAS'

Heat your oven to 200°C, 400°F, gas mark 6.
To make a pizza, you will need:

Peel me, chop me!

Peel us, crush us!

1 onion

2 cloves of garlic

2 tablespoons of olive oil

400g (14oz) can of chopped tomatoes

a ciabatta or baguette bread

Slice me finely!

250g (9oz) of mozzarella cheese

Toppings of your choosing

ham

olives

pepperoni

salami

cherry tomatoes

1. Gently heat the onion and garlic in the oil, until soft.

2. Mix in the tomatoes and some ground black pepper. Turn up the heat a little.

3. Heat the mixture until it boils, then reduce the heat and let it bubble.

Heat me until most of the liquid has gone.

4. Carefully cut the bread in half and place it on a baking tray.

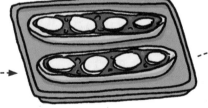

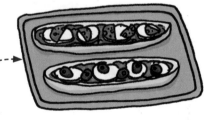

Spread the bread with the mixture...

...add the cheese...

...and any toppings.

5. Bake the pizzas for about 15 minutes. Carefully lift them out of the oven. Let them cool for 5 minutes, then cut them up...

STARS OF THE FUTURE

It's the first day of a TV talent show audition and lots of hopefuls have turned up to try their luck. Can you spot the following? Then, fill them in...

☆ three ballerinas in tutus

☆ a magician chasing an escaped rabbit

☆ a performing dog

☆ a boy band

☆ a guitarist

☆ a juggler

☆ a camera crew

☆ four people in striped tops

☆ an interviewer

☆ a group of cheerleaders

SUPERSTAR LIFE

If you were famous, what do you think your life would be like? What would you be?

A singer in a girl band?

A ballerina?

A movie star?

A brilliant scientist?

Imagine that you're being interviewed by a magazine. How would you answer the questions below?

I'd be... A movie star

I'd live in... Connecticut

I'd eat... pizza, watermelon, grapes, chocolate and popcorn candy

☆ Describe yourself in three words... AWESOME, Kind, lovable

☆ Who's your best friend and why? Vivi and lily because their fun, nice and loyal also Sydney and Lydan

☆ Which movie do you like best? Harry Potter the 3rd

☆ What are your hobbies? Swimming, soccer and I like to color and hang out with friends

Doodle hats and sunglasses on these celebrities to help them avoid the photographers who are always chasing them.

What to wear?

On the line

It's a good day for drying clothes. The sun is shining and a breeze is blowing, but all is not in order...

Some of the socks have lost their pairs. Circle the odd socks.

Knitting patterns

Priya loves to knit. She's knitting a scarf that follows a tricky pattern. Draw the correct number of green and purple dots in the final two sections.

Design a T-shirt

Use pens or pencils to decorate this T-shirt.

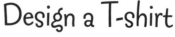

Flora loves flowery patterns, but hates wearing purple or green. Which item of clothes belongs to her? Circle her clothes.

Doodle

more socks on the washing line.

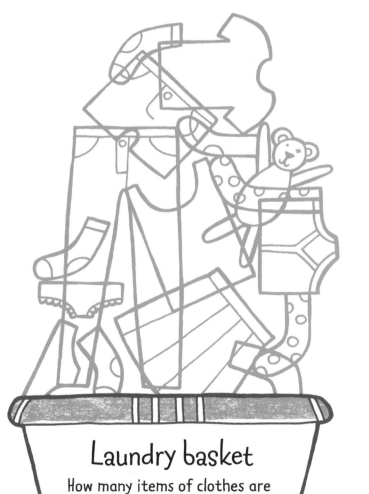

Laundry basket

How many items of clothes are piled up in this picture?

In a spin

Can you sort out the jumbled words below?

1. _ _ _ _ _   2. _ _ _ _ _ _ _ _

3. _ _ _ _ _ _ _ _   4. _ _ _ _ _

5. _ _ _ _ _ _ _ _ _ _ _ _ _

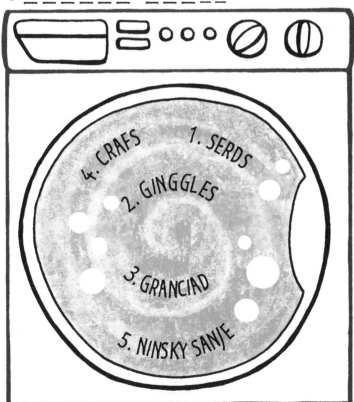

4. CRAFS   1. SERDS

2. GINGGLES

3. GRANCIAD

5. NINSKY SANJE

19

IT'S SNOWING!

WINTRY WORD GAME

The letters that make up these wintry words are all mixed up – can you put them in the correct order and find the words?

lownlabs ....

slevog ....

celici ....

strof ....

wamonns ....

frasc ....

zonerf ....

Which penguin catches the biggest fish?

A. B. C. D.

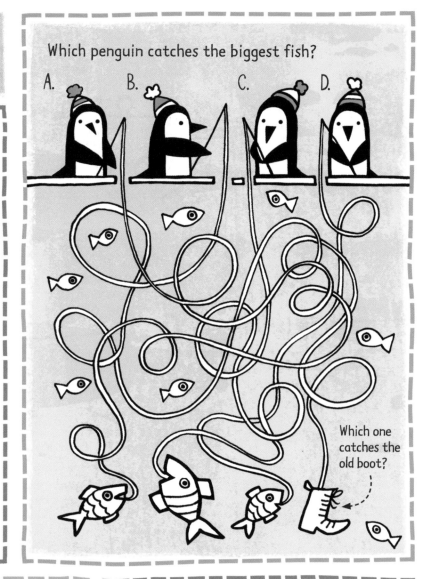

Which one catches the old boot?

POLAR BEAR TWINS

Which two of these polar bears are identical?

A clue: they may be facing in opposite directions.

SNOWBALL SUMS

In this puzzle, the number on each snowball is the sum of the two it's sitting on. Can you work out what the missing numbers are?

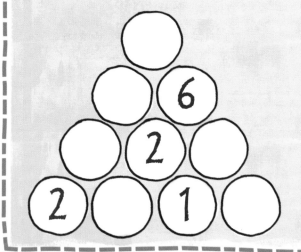

Fill in the people who are wearing hats.

How many birds can you spot? Fill them in and add some more.

Doodle more people in the snow.

TRUE OR FALSE? No two snowflakes are ever exactly the same shape.

Fairy woodland

Deep in the woods, the fairies and their friends come out to play. Decorate the scene with stickers from the middle of the book.

PINK MONSTER MAYHEM

Use the following ideas to fill the pages with
lots of monsters. Some could be friendly,
others could be pretty.

Fill in these monsters,
then doodle some more.

Spots...

Turn these spots into different monsters.

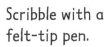

Draw some more in the spaces, too.

...and scribbles

Scribble with a felt-tip pen.

Then, doodle faces and body parts in black.

STREET LIFE

Draw some faces in the windows, and pretty flowers in pots.
Add numbers on the front doors, then fill in the picture.

Which house?

There's a birthday party today - can you work out which house it is being held at?

☆ It has a number on the door.
☆ It isn't next door to the pink house.
☆ It has a chimney on its roof.

☆ The people who live next door have a cat.
☆ The owners have a car parked in front.
☆ There are trees in pots outside the house.

Help this girl to find her way home, avoiding all the obstacles on the way.

Doodle more birds along the wires.

Around the world

Can you figure out which countries and continents these are?

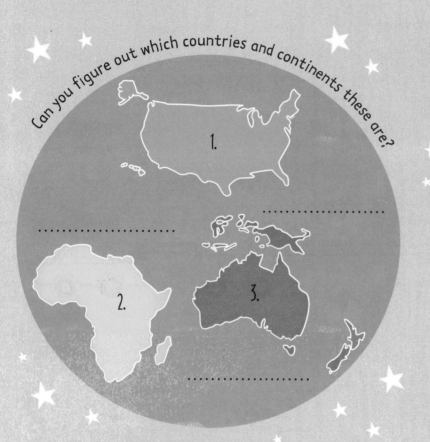

1.

2.

3.

Add pretty patterns and designs to this luggage

Doodle

hats, sunglasses, and other things to turn these blobs into tourists.

Passports

All these passports have a matching partner, except for one. Draw lines to link the pairs. Draw a circle around the odd one out.

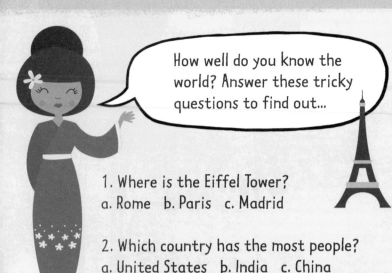

How well do you know the world? Answer these tricky questions to find out...

1. Where is the Eiffel Tower?
a. Rome   b. Paris   c. Madrid

2. Which country has the most people?
a. United States   b. India   c. China

3. Which of these deserts is the biggest?
a. The Sahara   b. The Arabian   c. The Gobi

4. What is the world's tallest man-made structure?
a. Tokyo Sky Tree   b. Warsaw Radio Tower
c. Burj Khalifa skyscraper

5. In which country do people eat tapas?
a. Spain   b. Germany   c. Hungary

6. Where do penguins live?
a. Iceland   b. The Arctic   c. Antarctica.

7. In which country do people wear kimonos?
a. India b. Japan c. Thailand

8. Where are the Niagara Falls?
a. Canada   b. U.S.A.   c. Both

Rockpool maze

Can you help this girl find her way to the sea? Watch out for the rockpools...

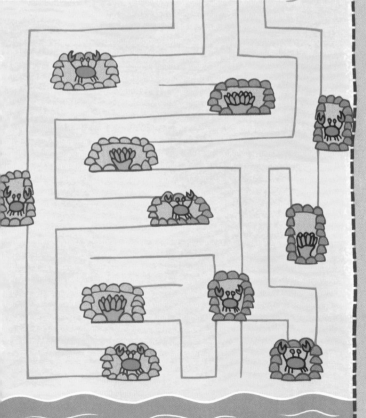

Luggage muddle

The country names on these luggage labels are mixed up. Can you put the letters in the correct order?

AIDIN
....

ENFARC
....

TULAASIAR
....

IXMCEO
....

NTILRAZSDWE
....

NKYAE
....

LNHAATDI
....

Pretty patterns

Doodle more patterns...

FUN AND GAMES

RANDOM PICTURE

Think of five random objects and write them below:

1. ....
2. ....
3. ....

4. ....
5. ....

Then, draw a picture including everything on your list.

princess... butterfly... strawberry... feather... ballet shoes...

SQUIGGLE PICTURES

Close your eyes and draw a squiggle or shape in the space below. Then, open your eyes and turn the squiggle into a picture of something.

For example, these squiggles could become...

a bird or a whale   a flower

QUEEN OF THE CASTLE

1. Draw a big circle on the ground with chalk, big enough for everyone to stand inside. This is the castle.

2. One person is the Queen. The Queen gives orders to everyone else, such as...

By order of the Queen, you shall hop on your left foot.

3. If anyone disobeys, they have to leave the castle. If the Queen gives an order without saying 'By order of the Queen' first, anyone who obeys has to leave the castle. The last person left, apart from the Queen, becomes the new Queen.

SHADOW TAG

1. On a sunny day...

'It'

...one person is 'it'. They try to 'tag' everyone else by stepping on their shadows.

2. If someone is tagged, they are out.

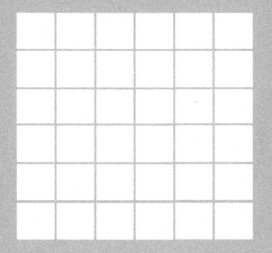

3. Once the last person is out, the one who was tagged first is 'it'.

SUN & MOON

One person draws a sun ☼ in a square on the board. The next person draws a moon ☽. The two players keep taking turns. The first person to make a vertical, horizontal or diagonal line of four symbols is the winner.

WHO AM I?

1. One person chooses a famous character from a book, movie or TV show.

Cinderella

2. They give a clue about the character, and everyone else takes turns guessing who it is.

I am in a fairy tale.

Are you Snow White?

Are you Rapunzel?

3. If someone guesses correctly, it is their turn to think of a character. If no one guesses, they are given another clue.

I lose a glass slipper.

You're Cinderella!

4. Play until someone guesses the character.

Animal magic

Transform these animals' heads by doodling their faces:

☆ add noses   ☆ doodle eyes   ☆ add mouths   ☆ and draw whiskers

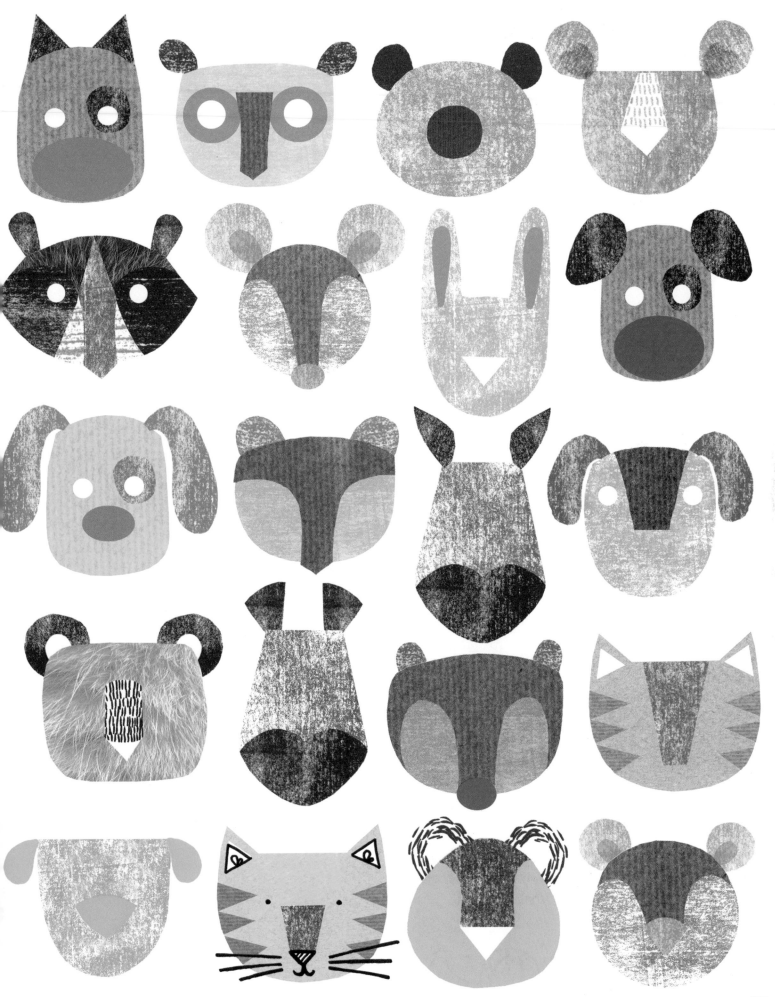

Summery seaside

Can you find a way through this maze to the beach?

Start here...

DID YOU KNOW?

Sand is made from tiny pieces of broken shell and rock.

THE BEACH

Fill in these little pictures with bright pens or pencils, if you like...

Strawberry sundae

To make a yummy strawberry sundae, you will need:

five or six strawberries, with the stalks removed

1 tablespoon of icing (powdered) sugar

vanilla or strawberry ice cream

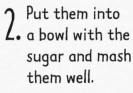

1. Rinse the strawberries and cut them in half.

2. Put them into a bowl with the sugar and mash them well.

3. Scoop some balls of ice cream and put them into a tall glass. Then, pour on the strawberry sauce.

Scatter strawberries, blueberries or raspberries over the top.

Here are 15 things that you might find at the seaside. Look really closely at them, then shut the book. Write down as many as you can remember.

Which of the middle pebbles is bigger?

Busy bee

The bee on the opposite page has been buzzing around, visiting lots of flowers. Add more flowers, then draw a line, without taking your pen off the paper, to show where the bee's been buzzing.

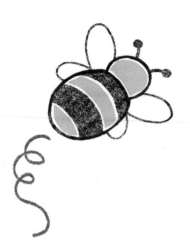

Fairy fun
Draw a fairy

Draw a head,
body and wings.

Add her face,
hair and crown.

Next, draw her
arms and legs.

Give the fairy
a magic wand.

Doodle
more flowers and fairies.

Fairy sandwiches

To make three sandwiches, you will need:

6 slices of bread

soft butter

a large round cutter and a small shaped cutter

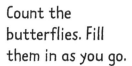

yummy spreads and fillings

1. Cut a circle from each slice of bread.

Chopping board

2. Then, cut a shape from three of the circles.

3. Spread butter on one side of each bread circle.

4. Spread a filling on top of each whole bread circle...

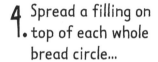

...then put the circles with the holes on top.

Count the butterflies. Fill them in as you go.

Total:

. . . .

Circle the five differences between these two fairy pictures:

Shopping trip

Help these friends to find a way from the bus stop to 'Fancy Feet', grabbing a chocolate cake on the way.

Shopping list code

Someone's dropped this list on the ground, but it's more mysterious than it appears, as there's a message hidden in it. Can you decode the message?

Clue: look carefully at the number next to each item, as it may help you to crack the code.

5 cream cakes
5 apples
4 cheeses
3 hats
2 pairs of socks
5 tomatoes
3 bottles of water
2 chocolate bars
2 pens
1 fish
2 notepads

1 umbrella
4 oranges
4 nectarines
3 scarves
3 chicken legs
3 pencils
2 magazines
1 tart
3 potatoes
1 egg
3 bananas

Write the message here:

Beautiful Boutique

Fill this boutique with clothes, hats and bags...

Decorate the lamp and the seat, if you like.

You could add more shoes, too.

AT THE ZOO

It's a busy day at the zoo. Can you solve the puzzle in each enclosure? There are things to count and spot too:

☆ Count the blue butterflies...

☆ See if you can find an escaped penguin.

These monkeys want to get to the bananas, but which way does each monkey need to go?

MONKEYS

FLAMINGOS

How many flamingos can you see here?

ELEPHANTS

The elephants need to get clean, but does their keeper have enough water? This is what you need to know:

• The black buckets are full, but the green ones are only half full.
• It takes 5 buckets to wash the green elephant.
• It takes 4 buckets to wash the purple elephant.
• It takes 2 buckets to wash the blue elephant.

Is there enough water? ......NO......

PENGUINS

The penguins' pool needs more water. Their keeper's come to do it, but his hoses are in a terrible mess. Which hose should he use?

B

LIONS

To reveal the lion in this picture, fill each shape with a yellow dot in it with a yellow pen, each shape with an orange dot with an orange pen, and so on.

KOALAS

This koala eats three eucalyptus leaves every hour, and it eats for five hours a day.

How many days will the leaves on this tree feed the koala for?

Circle the leaves as you count them, and make any calculations in this space:

$5 \times 3 = 15$

TIGERS

Find and circle two tigers that are exactly the same.

New worlds

Doodle a world on each
of these planets...

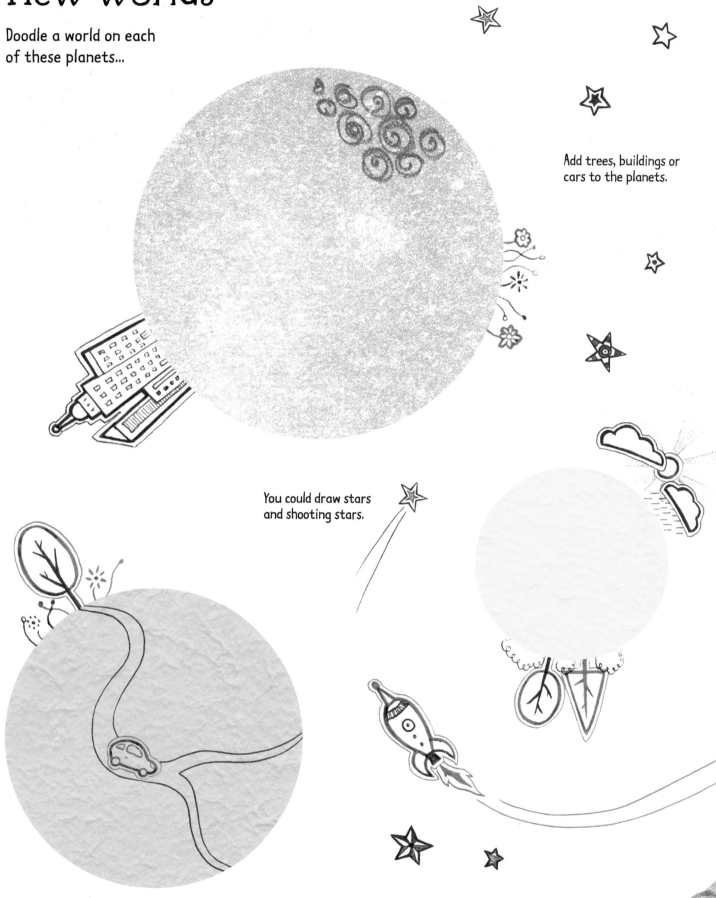

Add trees, buildings or
cars to the planets.

You could draw stars
and shooting stars.

Doodle flying saucers
or rockets, too.

Cupcake stand

Fill this cake stand with the stickers of cupcakes in the middle of the book, and add some tasty toppings.

HAUNTED HOUSE

Decorate this house with spooky stickers
from the sticker pages.

49

Under the sea

Doodle
more fish, shells
and seaweed.

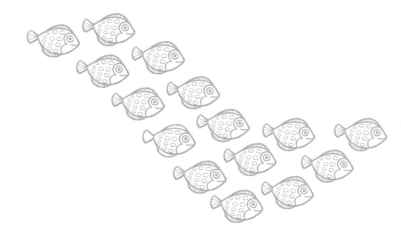

Hungry shark puzzle

How many fish does this hungry shark catch on its way to the coral? Going from square to square, follow the directions below. Fill in the squares and cross off the letters as you go:

R R U R D D L L D D R D L L D D L D R R R

(U=up   D=down   L=left   R=right)

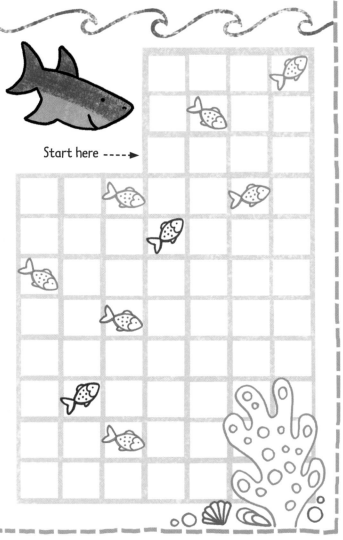

Start here ----►

DID YOU KNOW?

A dolphin breathes through a hole on its head. It swims to the surface, breathes out and then breathes in again.

Some fish swim in a group, so that other fish may think that they are one big fish.

Jellyfish don't have bones... or a brain.

Octopus tentacle tangle

Which tentacles belong to each octopus? To find out, fill them in, using a different pen for each octopus.

DIVING TALK

Under the water, divers use hand signals to tell each other things:

'Ok'

'Stop' or 'wait'

'I'm going up'

SECRET MEETING

Chloe's friend wants to meet her in town and has given Chloe directions using secret symbols. Can you find the meeting spot, following the symbols in the list?

Begin Chloe's journey at the START. Keep moving until she comes to a new intersection. The next symbol in the list will show her which way to go.

 = Straight on

= Turn left

= Turn right

TIP: Cross off each symbol as you come to an intersection, to keep track of where you are in the journey.

 START

Chloe's list of directions

Movies

52

Palace ball

These dancing princesses are wearing their most gorgeous gowns to the ball. Add more pretty patterns to the dresses.

Doodle
more hearts, stars and swirls.

CHOCOLATE!

Chocolate-box puzzle

'Eat' your way across this box, following the sequence below. You can go up or down, left or right, but not diagonally, and you have to finish in the bottom right corner. You can only 'eat' each chocolate in the box once!

Start here...

When you've finished the puzzle, you could fill it in, too...

Chocolate conundrum

Draw lines to link up the pairs of chocolates that are the same, and find one that doesn't have a pair:

Mmmm... milkshake

You will need:

a scoop of chocolate ice cream

a glass of chilled milk

a fork, for mixing

Beat the ice cream into the milk, until the milkshake's all smooth and frothy.

Drink me now!

56

CHOCOLATE SUNDAE

To make a delicious chocolate sundae, you will need:

 2 tablespoons of water

 100g (4oz) of plain (or milk) chocolate drops or chips

 *Vanilla!* ...*or chocolate!* ice cream

 15g (1 tablespoon) butter

 2 tablespoons of golden (corn) syrup

1. Melt the ingredients (apart from the ice cream!) on a low heat. Carefully lift the pan off the heat.

Stir us all the time!

2. Put some scoops of ice cream into a tall glass.

3. Pour the chocolate sauce over the ice cream.

 TASTY TIP To make your sundae even MORE chocolatey, carefully grate some chocolate, then sprinkle it over the top.

Chocolate trees

Chocolate grows on trees... (well, kind of)

 Cacao trees... ...grow fruit called pods.

In the pods are seeds called cocoa beans.

The beans are roasted and crushed, making cocoa powder and cocoa butter...

...which combine to make chocolate!

DID YOU KNOW?

The scientific name for chocolate is Theobroma cacao, which means 'food of the gods' in Greek.

57

SEEING THINGS

Dazzling dots

There's an animal or bird hiding here – can you see what it is? Fill in each shape with a red dot in it with a red pen, each shape with a green dot with a green pen, and so on. But, don't use a black pen for the shapes with black spots.

Bug pairs

Fill in each pair of these bugs. Which one is left on its own?

Busy slopes

A girl is looking at the ski slopes through a viewing telescope, but which is the view she can see? Only one of the views below is taken from the picture on the right. Which one is it?

A.

B.

C.

D.

View .... is correct.

Changing shapes puzzle

Fold a paper square in half, three times:

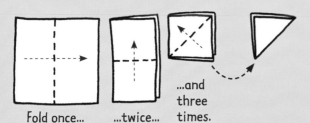

Fold once...   ...twice...   ...and three times.

Cut the shapes below out of it...

...then open it out, and you'll make this!

Looking at the folded shapes below, can you work out which one makes each opened-out shape?

Link each pair with a line, and if you can't work any of them out, try making them:

In the garden

Flowers are blooming in this country garden.
Decorate the pages with lots of bug stickers
from the sticker pages.

French fashion

These ladies and gentlemen are wearing their most elegant outfits. Circle everything you can spot, then fill in the clothes.

Can you find someone with a parasol?

There are three rose bushes – can you find them?

Can you spot fifteen ladies wearing feathers?

Can you see six men wearing hats?

Can you spot five dogs?

There are eight couples holding hands. Can you spot them all?

Can you find thirteen open fans?

63

Birthday brain benders

You'll need a pencil and an eraser for these tricky puzzles.

You've received an invitation to a birthday party. Can you draw over the envelope without taking your pencil off the paper or going over any of your lines twice?

Seven girls would like some birthday cake, but you're only allowed to cut it three times. Can you divide this cake into seven pieces, using just three straight lines?

Hint: the pieces don't have to be the same size.

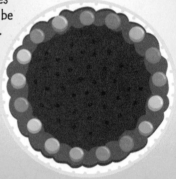

See how many words you can make from the word:

decorations

For each new word, you can only use the letters as many times as they appear. Write your words here:

Pass the present

Can you move (not remove) one present to turn this arrangement of presents into a plus shape (+) with six gifts in each row?

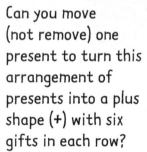

Sisters Ruby and Jenna are identical twins. At their birthday party, Mia asks them how old they are.

How can this be?

A birthday girl is nine years old today. Can you put the numbers 1 to 9 into the balloons, so that each line adds up to seventeen?

Spot the difference

There are lots of birthday gifts below, but some things are missing from the picture on the right. Can you spot what they are? Fill in the pictures once you've found what's missing.

Princess fun

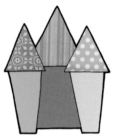

1. Glue down three wonky rectangles and three triangles.

2. Add wavy strips to the roofs, hearts for the windows, and a door.

3. Glue on some sequins and draw a heart and some flags on the roofs.

66

Tangled hair maze

Which princess will find a brave knight?

A. B. C. D.

Princess search

Can you find these princess words hidden in the wordsearch? They could be vertical, horizontal, diagonal, or even back to front.

~~tiara~~ ~~gown~~
~~jewel~~ ~~tower~~
~~palace~~ ~~throne~~
~~prince~~ ~~carriage~~

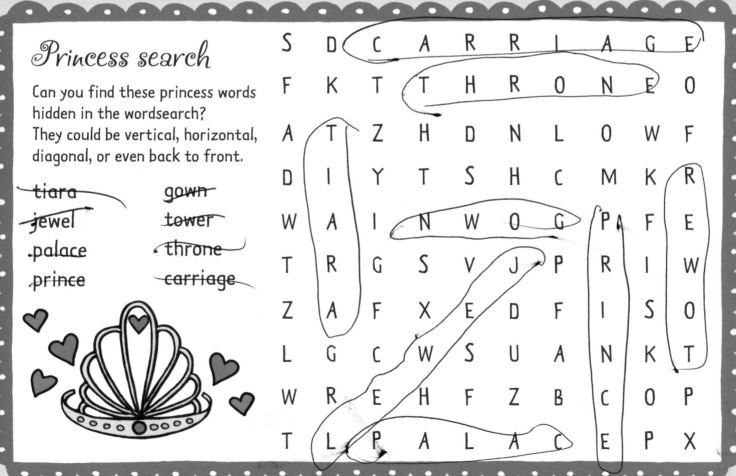

S	D	C	A	R	R	I	A	G	E
F	K	T	T	H	R	O	N	E	O
A	T	Z	H	D	N	L	O	W	F
D	I	Y	T	S	H	C	M	K	R
W	A	I	N	W	O	G	P	F	E
T	R	G	S	V	J	P	R	I	W
Z	A	F	X	E	D	F	I	S	O
L	G	C	W	S	U	A	N	K	T
W	R	E	H	F	Z	B	C	O	P
T	L	P	A	L	A	C	E	P	X

Doodle hearts...

You could draw
hearts within
hearts.

Doodle patterns
in some...

...and simply
fill in others.

...and flowers!

Draw a simple flower shape with a dot for a middle.

Add spots on some flowers...

Fill in others.

...and doodle little leaves.

At the ballet

This scene from The Nutcracker shows the Sugar Plum Fairy dancing with her Cavalier in the magical land of sweets.

Fill in the dancers and the stage set.

Ballet positions

These are the basic ballet positions. Try them for yourself.

First position   Second position   Third position   Fourth position   Fifth position

Drawing a ballerina

Draw a head. Add a body and fluffy tutu below.

Add hair and a tiara.

Draw a face.

Draw legs and arms then fill her in.

Draw your own dancing ballerinas here...

Spy girls

Things that every spy girl should have in her wardrobe...

Hat to disguise hair

Sunglasses to hide face

Dark clothing to blend into the shadows

Watch, to be on time for secret meetings

Running shoes to creep around in

Secret signs

You can pass secret messages to your friends using gestures. You could make up your own gestures and meanings, too.

'We're being spied on.'

'Meet me in the secret place.'

'Follow me.'

'Keep away.'

Spy maze

Help this spy girl get through the park without meeting anyone.

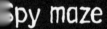

Code cracking

To send a secret message to a friend, use this reverse code:

- Write your message
- Split it into random groups of letters. For example,
  'Meet you at the gate' could be written:

  MEE TY OUAT TH EGA TE

- Then, write each group back to front:

  EEM YT TAUO HT AGE ET

....

....

....

Can you crack this reverse code message?

EGRAT ATST SAHR CITON EMDE
ILIAT EHGN SR MAIO NIOG NIG
DIHOT GNI. OYFI AWU TN POT
PUKCI HT ARTE LI, IEHS ATSS
AGNIY HTT NARGE OHD LET.
NOD TO CTEG THGUA!

Doodle faces on these fingerprints.

In the crowd

Aisha needs to pass a secret message to her 'contact', but she doesn't know what the contact looks like. She only has the following information:

☆ The contact is wearing a hat.　　☆ The contact is carrying a bag.
☆ The contact is wearing something yellow.

At the movies

A Hollywood star is walking down the red carpet at a movie premiere. Fill in her gown, then add some accessories, too.

On location

This movie scene is set in a grand old house and is being filmed over two days. Everything should be identical... but it's not. Can you spot five things out of place on Tuesday?

MONDAY

TUESDAY

Costume department

The costume department has lent out some 1920s accessories but they've been returned with parts missing. Spot the missing parts and fill them in.

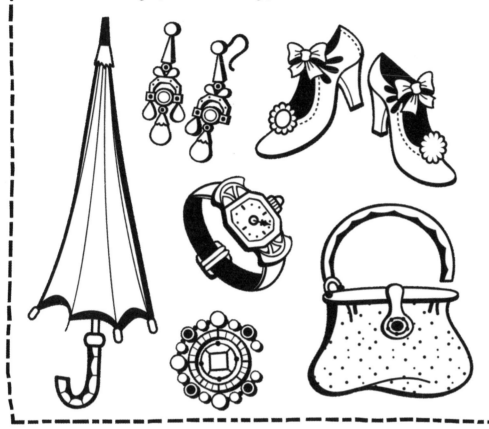

In makeup

Style this actress' hair and apply her makeup.

What kind of movie do you think she's in?

Movie mix-up

The shots from this movie are mixed up. Can you put them in the correct order?

Write numbers 1-5 in the circles.

FINISH THE STORY

Every story has a beginning, a middle and an end. But so far, this story only has a beginning. Write your own middle and end by adding what you think should happen next.

← Add a title for your story

Before you start writing, ask yourself...

● What does the princess see inside the mysterious cottage?

● Who lives there? Who does the voice belong to?

● What's making the glowing red light and what does the inside of the cottage look like?

● What happens when the princess goes inside?

● Does Princess Rose find her way home in the end?

● If she gets home, has anyone missed her? Are people angry, or glad she's back?

There once was a princess named Rose. One summer evening, she went out for a ride on her pony. The sun set more quickly than she thought it would and she soon found herself lost in the forest.

Suddenly, she saw a cottage up ahead. Its roof was thatched with straw and its windows glowed red. The door creeeeaked open, and a high-pitched, croaky voice told her to come in. Princess Rose couldn't resist. She jumped off her pony and tiptoed inside where she saw...

Continue the story →

_____

_____

_____

_____

_____

Here are some words that you could use in your story, if you like...

silent SPELL   ancient   MOON
charms   DAZZLING
evil gnarled   eerie   enchanted
curse   shadowy   glow   gloomy
    frog   cruel WHISPER
magic potion   prince   WOLF

Doodle more
decorations
around the
border.

Numbers, numbers

On your marks...

In this race, the girls successfully jump over hurdles marked with correct equations, but knock down any incorrect ones. Cross out the equations with the wrong answers. Then, write in who jumps over the most hurdles and wins.

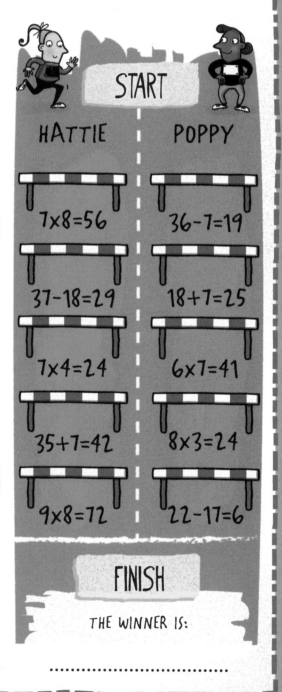

START

HATTIE   **POPPY**

$7 \times 8 = 56$ $36 - 7 = 19$

$37 - 18 = 29$ $18 + 7 = 25$

$7 \times 4 = 24$ $6 \times 7 = 41$

$35 + 7 = 42$ $8 \times 3 = 24$

$9 \times 8 = 72$ $22 - 17 = 6$

FINISH

THE WINNER IS:

....

Balancing act

Can you balance the totals of these toppling trays? Take away three boxes from the orange tray and draw them on the blue tray instead.

Cross-number

Solve the clues and write the correct numbers in the grid.

Across →

1. Two times five thousand and fifteen

4. Two hundred and thirty seven, backwards

6. What is one hundred times eleven?

Down ↓

2. Write the number three hundred and seven thousand, six hundred and two.

3. Five thousand plus two thousand, two hundred and nineteen

5. How many legs do fifty cats have?

Monkey puzzle

The monkey can only reach his friend by climbing past the equations with answers that are even numbers. Write in the answers, then his route.

FINISH

$8+3+1$
= ......

5×7
= ....

$7+15$
= ....

$24+4+3$
= ......

2×4
= ....

9×9
= ....

6×6
= ....

$9+8+3$
= ......

$12+14$
= ......

$3+9+1=$......

6×8
= ....

$2+7+9$
= ......

START

Fold it!

It's very difficult to fold most pieces of paper, whatever their size, in half and half again, and again, more than seven or eight times.

Try it for yourself, and then challenge your friends too.

Spotted dogs

Use the clues to work out how many spots each dog has. Draw them on, and circle the dog with the most spots.

Clue 1. Monty has as many spots as Penny and Daisy put together.

Clue 2. Daisy has twice as many spots as Penny, and three times as many as Millie.

Penny = 3

Monty = ...

Daisy = ...

Millie = ...

79

Animal fun

Parrot pairs

Spot the identical pairs of parrots.
Fill in each pair to match.

Stand up giraffes

1. Draw half a giraffe on a folded rectangle of thick paper.

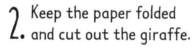

2. Keep the paper folded and cut out the giraffe.

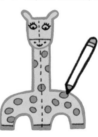

3. Fold its head over, then decorate it.

Hungry snails

Which of these snails munched on the tasty leaf?

A.   B.   C.   D.

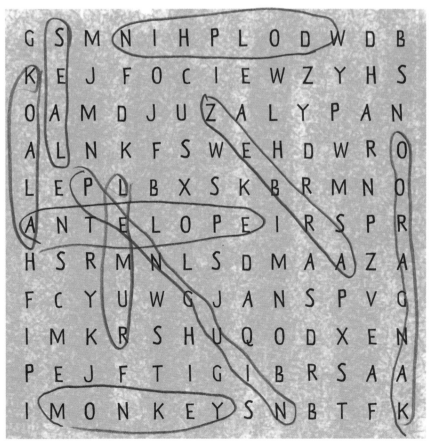

Animal wordsearch

Can you find all the animal names hidden in this wordsearch? They might run horizontally, vertically, diagonally, or even backwards...

ANTELOPE	KANGAROO	MONKEY
DOLPHIN	LEMUR	PENGUIN
SEAL	ZEBRA	KOALA

DID YOU KNOW?

Pandas spend up to 16 hours a day eating bamboo.

```
G S M N I H P L O D W D B
K E J F O C I E W Z Y H S
O A M D J U Z A L Y P A N
A L N K F S W E H D W R O
L E P L B X S K B R M N O
A N T E L O P E I R S P R
H S R M N L S D M A A Z A
F C Y U W G J A N S P V G
I M K R S H U Q O D X E N
P E J F T I G I B R S A A
I M O N K E Y S N B T F K
```

PLAYFUL PENGUINS

This icy landscape needs more penguins! Add lots of
stickers from the sticker pages of penguins playing
on the ice and swimming in the sea.

Enchanted forest

Magical story

Add some magical words to complete this fairytale.

Deep in the heart of an enchanted forest lived a beautiful fairy named................ She loved to sing, but there was a big, mean................in the forest who didn't like her singing! He always roared loudly to drown her out, which made................feel very................ She decided to teach him a lesson. One night, she crept over to him while he was sleeping in his ...., and began to sing loudly. He woke up and started to roar. Suddenly, the fairy flew up and pushed some sticky .... into his mouth. The angry................'s mouth was stuck, so .... was free to sing all day long.

Draw a unicorn

1. Draw a body, head and legs.

2. Add a mane and tail.

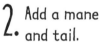

3. Draw wings, a face and a horn.

85

Get a clue...

A clever detective never misses a good clue. Do you always notice what's going on around you?
Here are some handy tips, and some mysteries for you to solve:

Detective tips

Wear plain clothes that blend in, so
that you don't stand out.

Look everywhere
for clues – anything
could be relevant.

Train yourself to remember
people's faces. You might need
to spot them later on.

Train tunnel mystery

While this train was passing through a tunnel, some pranksters struck and changed things around.
Use your powers of observation to spot the 15 changes. Some things have been moved, some have
been added or replaced and some have gone missing.

 BEFORE

AFTER

Naughty pups

Molly's gone upstairs to find that one of her dogs has left muddy paw prints all over her room. Study the crime scene, suspects and clues. Which dog is the culprit?

THE SCENE OF THE CRIME

CHI-CHI

THE SUSPECTS

CHESTER   SALLY   ROSIE   CHI-CHI   BERTIE

THE CLUES

1) Bertie knows that he isn't allowed on Molly's bed.

2) Whenever Chester goes into Molly's room, he hides all her socks under the bed.

3) Only the four smaller dogs are allowed upstairs.

4) Sally doesn't like to climb up on chairs.

CHI-CHI

All steamed up

The hair salon is empty. Its owner is missing.

The only clue is some writing on a steamed-up mirror. Can you work out where she is?

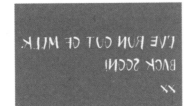

....

87

A trip through time

Imagine you're going on a very special journey... in a time machine. You'll be visiting a few different places and times in history, so you'll need to pack the correct clothes. Here are some outfits from different times. Fill them in, then design an outfit that you think will be fashionable in the future.

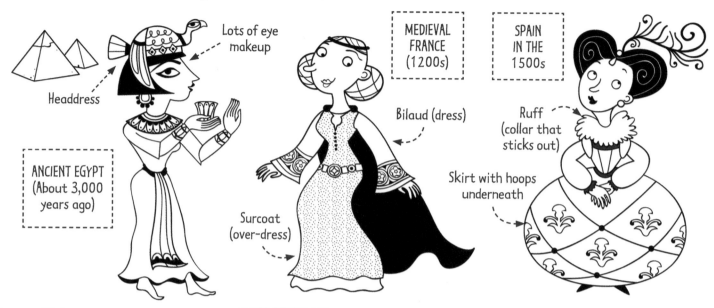

Lots of eye makeup

Headdress

ANCIENT EGYPT (About 3,000 years ago)

MEDIEVAL FRANCE (1200s)

SPAIN IN THE 1500s

Bilaud (dress)

Surcoat (over-dress)

Ruff (collar that sticks out)

Skirt with hoops underneath

Doodle

curls and decorations to create more fancy hairstyles.

Some wealthy ladies in the 1700s wore elaborate hairstyles like this.

JAPAN IN THE 1800s

ENGLAND IN THE 1920s

Tight fitting cloche hat

Design your own **future outfit**

Wrap-around dress called a kimono

Did you KNOW?

In the late 1800s many women wore tight corsets under their clothes to give them tiny waists.

Oh my!

Corset

The laces were pulled to make the corset tighter.

Sometimes they were so tight that women fainted.

Fun things to do when you travel in time

Nice to meet you

Meet people from history that you've learned about at school and see what they're really like.

Meet your grandmother as a little girl and see what things were like for her growing up.

Travel to the future and see what people will be wearing.

?

See what you look like in the future.

Try out food from different times in the past and decide which is the tastiest.

Go back in time to listen to a famous group's first concert.

Magical mermaids

Draw patterns on these mermaids' tails...

...and on their tops, too.

Add a bracelet or necklace...

...then fill in all the mermaids!

Cut-and-stick mermaid

1. Draw a mermaid's face and arms.

2. Add her body and hair.

3. Draw a top and a tail on patterned paper. Cut them out...

4. ...and glue them onto your drawing.

Use giftwrap, or paper cut from an old magazine.

You could use shining paper for her tail, if you have some.

Mermaid friends puzzle

Look carefully at the four pictures of each kind of sea creature – can you see the odd one out? Draw a circle around each one that's different.

(One of them has been done, to start you off.)

This starfish has fewer spots than the others.

Can you spot five differences between these two pictures? Circle each one as you find it...

Answers and solutions

2-3 IN THE PARK

Sunglasses: ⭕
Red spotted dresses: ⭕
Taking photos: ⭕
Red balloon: ⭕

Cyclists: ⭕
Beach balls: ⭕
Dogs: ⭕

6-7 FUN IN THE RAIN

SHOPPING LIST PUZZLE:
dreba = bread,   kilm = milk,   eshece = cheese,
telucte = lettuce,   aanabn = banana

COUNT THE RAINDROPS:
There are 142 raindrops.

PUDDLE-JUMPING:

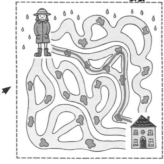

8-9 SPARKLING JEWELS

STOP, THIEF!:

MISSING BEADS:

CROWNS PUZZLE: C

PRINCESS PUZZLE: Jess = 15,   Bella = 10,   Izzy = 5

GEMS WORDSEARCH:

12-13 PRINCESS RESCUE MAZE

14-15 FOODY FUN

FOOD MIX-UP:
yehon = honey,   smoteota = tomatoes,
lurof = flour,   skieoco = cookies,
arclee = cereal,   tapsa = pasta

16-17 STARS OF THE FUTURE

Ballerinas in tutus: ⭕
Magican and rabbit: ⭕
Performing dog: ⭕
Boy band: ⭕
Guitarist: ⭕

Juggler: ⭕
Camera crew: ⭕
Striped tops: ⭕
Interviewer: ⭕
Cheerleaders: ⭕

18-19 WHAT TO WEAR?

ON THE LINE:

Odd socks: ○
Flora's clothes: ○

KNITTING PATTERNS: →

LAUNDRY BASKET:
There are fifteen pieces of clothing, plus one bear.

IN A SPIN:
1. Dress   2. Leggings
3. Cardigan   4. Scarf
5. Skinny jeans

20-21 IT'S SNOWING!

WINTRY WORD GAME:

lownlabs = snowball,   slevog = gloves,
celici = icicle,   strof = frost,   wamonns = snowman,
frasc = scarf,   zonerf = frozen

PENGUIN PUZZLE:
Penguin C catches the biggest fish.
Penguin B catches the old boot.

POLAR BEAR TWINS:

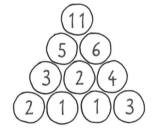

SNOWBALL SUMS:

```
      11
     5  6
    3  2  4
   2  1  1  3
```

TRUE OR FALSE? True

26-27 STREET LIFE

WAY HOME: →

WHICH HOUSE?:
The birthday party is at the yellow house.

28-29 AROUND THE WORLD

COUNTRIES AND CONTINENTS:
1. USA   2. Africa   3. Australasia

PASSPORTS:

ROCKPOOL MAZE:

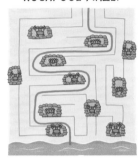

WORLD QUIZ:
1 = b,   2 = c,   3 = a,   4 = c,   5 = a,   6 = c,   7 = b,   8 = c

LUGGAGE MUDDLE:
AIDIN = INDIA,   ENFARC = FRANCE,   TULAASIAR = AUSTRALIA,
IXMCEO = MEXICO,   NTILRAZSDWE = SWITZERLAND,
LNHAATDI = THAILAND,   NKYAE = KENYA

36-37 SUMMERY SEASIDE

SEASIDE MAZE:

PEBBLE PUZZLE:
They are both the same size.

40-41 FAIRY FUN

BUTTERFLIES:
There are 57 butterflies.

SPOT THE DIFFERENCE:

42-43 SHOPPING TRIP

SHOPPING LIST CODE:
Meet at the fountain at ten.

44-45 AT THE ZOO

FLAMINGOS:
There are seven flamingos.

MONKEY MAZE:

TIGERS:

ELEPHANTS: No

PENGUINS: B

KOALAS: The leaves will last for four days.

THINGS TO SPOT:

Blue butterflies: 8 ◯ Escaped penguin: ◯

50-51 UNDER THE SEA

HUNGRY SHARK PUZZLE:
The shark catches six fish.

52-53 HIDDEN RENDEZVOUS

56-57 CHOCOLATE!

CHOCOLATE-BOX PUZZLE:

CHOCOLATE CONUNDRUM:

58-59 SEEING THINGS

DAZZLING DOTS:
It's a parrot.

BUG PAIRS:

BUSY SLOPES:
View D is correct.

CHANGING SHAPES PUZZLE:

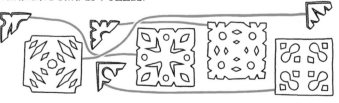

62-63 FRENCH FASHION

Parasol: ○   Hats: ○
Rose bushes: ○   Dogs: ○
Feathers: ○   Open fans: ○
Couples holding hands: ○

64-65 BIRTHDAY BRAIN BENDERS

ENVELOPE PUZZLE: CUT THE CAKE...:

DECORATIONS:
Some words you may have found = aid, race, core, ants, rides, drastic...

PASS THE PRESENT:
Move a box from the end of the row of six, and put it on top of the middle box. Now, both rows have six boxes in them.

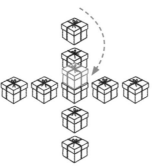

TWINS PUZZLE:
One twin was born five minutes before midnight, while the other twin was born five minutes after midnight.

BALLOONS: SPOT THE DIFFERENCE:

66-67 PRINCESS FUN

TANGLED HAIR MAZE: D
PRINCESS SEARCH:

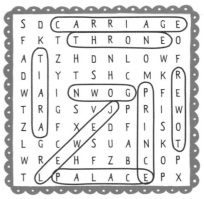

72-73 SPY GIRLS

SPY MAZE:

IN THE CROWD:

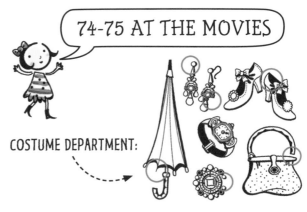

CODE CRACKING:
Target Star has noticed me tailing her so I am going into hiding. If you want to pick up the trail she is staying at the Grand Hotel. Do not get caught!

74-75 AT THE MOVIES

COSTUME DEPARTMENT:

74-75 AT THE MOVIES continued

ON LOCATION:

MOVIE MIX-UP:

3

1

2

5

4

78-79 NUMBERS, NUMBERS

ON YOUR MARKS...: The winner is Hattie.

BALANCING ACT:

MONKEY PUZZLE:

CROSS-NUMBER:

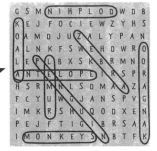

SPOTTED DOGS: Monty = 9, Daisy = 6, Milly = 2

80-81 ANIMAL FUN

PARROT PAIRS:

HUNGRY SNAILS: C

ANIMAL WORDSEARCH:

84-85 ENCHANTED FOREST

MYSTERIOUS MAZE:

You meet a FAIRY on the way.

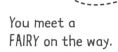

86-87 GET A CLUE...

TRAIN TUNNEL MYSTERY:

NAUGHTY PUPS:
Chi-chi is the culprit.

ALL STEAMED UP: The message reads:
I'VE RUN OUT OF MILK. BACK SOON! xx

90-91 MAGICAL MERMAIDS

MERMAID FRIENDS PUZZLE:

SPOT THE DIFFERENCE: